Pebble® Plus

Investigate the Seasons

Let's Look at Fall

Revised Edition

by Sarah L. Schuette

4D

Download the Capstone 4D app for additional content.

 See page 2 for directions.

CAPSTONE PRESS
a capstone imprint

Download the Capstone 4D app!

- Ask an adult to search in the Apple App Store or Google Play for "Capstone 4D".
- Click Install (Android) or Get, then Install (Apple).
- Open the app.
- Scan any of the following spreads with this icon:

When you scan a spread, you'll find fun extra stuff to go with this book!
You can also find these things on the web at www.capstone4D.com
using the password: **fall.08604**

Pebble Plus is published by Capstone Press,
1710 Roe Crest Drive, North Mankato, Minnesota 56003
www.mycapstone.com

Library of Congress Cataloging-in-Publication Data
is available on the Library of Congress website.

ISBN 978-1-5435-0860-4 (library binding)
ISBN 978-1-5435-0876-5 (paperback)
ISBN 978-1-5435-0880-2 (ebook pdf)

Editorial Credits
Sarah Bennett, designer; Tracy Cummins, media researcher,
Laura Manthe, production specialist

Photo Credits
Shutterstock: Dave Allen Photography, 7, DmZ, 5, Erik Mandre,
15, FotoRequest, 13, Grisha Bruev, 9, images72, 17, Liubou
Yasiukovich, Cover Design Element, Manamana, 11, Nancy Gill,
19, nikitsin.smugmug.com, 1, Piotr Krzeslak, Cover, Sofiaworld,
3, Victor Grow, 21

Note to Parents and Teachers

The Investigate the Seasons set supports national science
standards related to weather and life science. This book
describes and illustrates the season of fall. The images support
early readers in understanding the text. The repetition of words
and phrases helps early readers learn new words. This book also
introduces early readers to subject-specific vocabulary words,
which are defined in the Glossary section. Early readers may
need assistance to read some words and to use the Table of
Contents, Glossary, Read More, Internet Sites, Critical Thinking
Questions, and Index sections of the book.

Printed in the United States of America.
010773S18

Table of Contents

It's Fall!

How do you know it's fall?

A cool breeze blows.

The weather is colder.

Leaves change color.

They flutter to the ground.

The sun sets earlier.

Fall days are shorter

than summer days.

Animals in Fall

What do animals do in fall?

Squirrels rush around.

They gather nuts

to store for winter.

Birds fly south.

They look

for warmer weather.

13

Bears search for a place

to hibernate.

Their fur coats grow thicker.

Plants in Fall

What happens

to plants in fall?

Ripe apples fill the orchard.

They're ready to be picked.

Corn ripens in the field.

It's ready to be harvested.

19

What's Next?

The temperature grows cold.

Fall is over.

What season is next?

Glossary

breeze—a gentle wind

flutter—to wave, flap, or float in a breeze; leaves flutter as they drop off tree branches

harvest—to gather crops that are ready to be picked; fall is a time for harvesting crops such as corn, soybeans, wheat, and oats

hibernate—to spend the winter in a deep sleep

orchard—a field or farm where fruit trees grow

ripen—to become ready to be picked

season—one of the four parts of the year; winter, spring, summer, and fall are seasons

weather—the condition outdoors at a certain time and place; weather changes with each season

Read More

Appleby, Alex. *What Happens in Fall?* Four Super Seasons. New York: Gareth Stevens Pub., 2014.

Brennan, Linda Crotta. *Leaves Change Color.* Tell Me Why. Ann Arbor, Mich.: Cherry Lake Publishing, 2015.

Herrington, Lisa M. *How Do You Know it's Fall?* Rookie Read-About Science. New York: Children's Press, 2014.

Internet Sites

Use FactHound to find Internet sites related to this book.

Visit *www.facthound.com*

Just type 9781543508604 and go.

 Check out projects, games and lots more at
www.capstonekids.com

Critical Thinking Questions

1. Describe two signs that it is fall.

2. What do squirrels do in fall?

3. Describe what "harvest" means. Use the glossary to help you.

Index